THINGS THAT GROW

360 DEGREES
(an imprint of the Little Tiger Group)
1 The Coda Centre, 189 Munster Road,
London SW6 6AW
www.littletiger.co.uk
First published in Great Britain 2017
Text by Libby Walden
Text copyright © 2017 Caterpillar Books
Illustrated by Becca Stadtlander
Illustrations copyright © Becca Stadtlander 2017
All rights reserved • ISBN: 978-1-84857-525-7
Printed in China • CPB/1800/0582/0916
10 9 8 7 6 5 4 3 2 1

Written by Libby Walden • Illustrated by Becca Stadtlander

THINGS THAT GROW

INTRODUCTION

Plants, animals, humans and the features of our planet, such as rivers and islands, all develop and grow with every passing day. This book examines the processes that make the changing world so diverse and exciting, from the tiniest seed to the tallest mountain.

CONTENTS

PLANTS AND TREES

The plant kingdom is vast, with over 400,000 species worldwide,
from miniature mosses to gigantic redwood trees, and from
delicate poppies to vicious Venus fly-traps.

What ties them together is that they all start life as seeds or spores,
and we shall explore the remarkable journey these magical
little parcels undergo to become fully-formed plants and trees.

LIFE IN CYCLES

From small seeds grow large trees and from large trees
drop small seeds – plant life is in a constant cycle.

Under the right conditions,
a planted seed will sprout
roots and shoots in a
process called germination.

The roots will grow downwards in search
of nutrients and water, and the shoots
will grow upwards looking for light.

The shoots develop into a stem or trunk which will grow to stabilise the plant. From this, branches, leaves, and sometimes flowers and fruit will begin to sprout.

BARKING UP
THE WRONG TREE

The spongy inner bark transports sugar,
water and other nutrients gathered by
the roots to the rest of the tree.

The tree trunk is protected by
a hard coating called the outer
bark, which is made up of dried
cork-like cells.

Each year a tree will grow a new layer of wood around the outside of the trunk, under the bark. This new layer is called a growth ring.

When a tree has been cut down, you can usually tell its age by counting the number of rings on the trunk. Each ring marks one year, and the average lifespan of a tree is between 50 and 75 years.

PLANTING A SEED

There are a vast variety of seeds, from tiny to huge, delicate to sturdy and smooth to spiky. However, they all have one thing in common – the potential to grow into something much bigger.

———

From the twirling 'helicopters' of the sycamore to the hairy coconut of the exotic palm and from the decorative seed-carrying cone of the redwood to the spiky cases of the horse chestnut – all seeds are amazing starting points for life.

sycamore

coconut
palm

redwood

horse chestnut

WHAT PLANTS NEED TO GROW

All seeds need water, oxygen and the right temperature to start growing. Without these three things, a seed will not germinate and will just remain a seed.

Generally, once growth has started, a plant needs air, light, water, nutrients and space in order to grow tall and strong.

Most plants will take what they need from the surrounding environment but humans often help by watering plants when it has been a dry day or sprinkling fertiliser on the soil.

AIR-FRESHENERS

As well as providing food and shade for many animals, plants provide another important service – they clean the air!

Plants use light energy from the Sun to produce their food, known as glucose, in a process called photosynthesis. During photosynthesis, a plant takes carbon dioxide and water from the air through its pores (or stomata) and releases oxygen back into the atmosphere, recycling and cleaning the air.

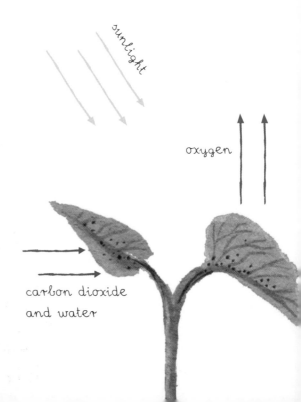

sunlight

oxygen

carbon dioxide and water

A LITTLE HELP FROM MY FRIENDS

Pollination is a very important part of the plant life cycle as it helps flowers to grow seeds and, in time, more flowers!

———

Insects (particularly bees), birds and the wind all help with this process by moving pollen from plant to plant, an act which then fertilises plant egg cells and creates seeds.

Pollen gets caught on the bees' legs and bodies.

17

UNDERNEATH THE PETALS

The centre of a flower is the reproductive powerhouse where seeds are made. Each flower has both male and female reproductive organs. Both are vital for the formation of seeds.

———

The anther in the male stamen creates the pollen grains that get carried from flower to flower by pollinating animals.

———

When an animal carrying pollen visits a flower, it is the female ovary that uses the pollen to fertilise the ovules and eventually turns the pollen grains into seeds.

Petals are brightly coloured
to attract pollinating insects.

SEEDS WILL TRAVEL

Some animals, such as squirrels, will collect and store seeds and nuts to help them survive the winter.

But if food is buried or if hiding places are forgotten, those winter stores will unexpectedly take root and grow into a new plant or tree!

Birds can be brilliant seed-carriers but their methods of distribution are not always glamorous! Sometimes berries are dropped in flight, but a more common method of dispersal is for undigested seeds to grow from bird poo.

The dandelion seed is a perfect little adventurer. Built like a parachute, it catches the wind as it falls from the seed head and is then carried away to pastures new.

EXTREME PLANTS

Some plants are able to grow and survive in the most extreme conditions on the planet.

Aquatic plants live a life submerged in water and have to work hard to collect enough sunlight to create food. Water lilies have large pads that float on the surface, with a waxy top layer that repels water in order to keep the stomata (gas-collecting pores) open.

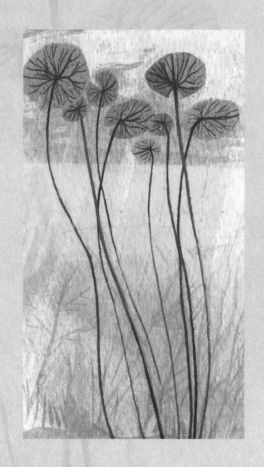

Desert plants have expertly adapted to survive in the driest places. Cacti have shallow roots, close to the surface, to collect rainwater, and they only open their stomata at night so the heat of the Sun doesn't evaporate any collected water. Their large, fleshy stems act as water-stores and they have a thick, waxy skin to reflect heat from the strong desert Sun.

HARDY SURVIVORS

Mountain plants have to be especially hardy to survive dramatic temperature changes, strong winds and unpredictable weather.

Gorse bushes are short, dense and flexible enough to bend with the wind, so they don't get uprooted and blown away when storms hit.

Some plants are unable to survive on their
own but have developed a clever and cunning trick in
order to stay alive – they latch on to a larger plant or
tree, using it as a 'host'.

These parasitic plants have modified roots that
connect and tap into the central food or water
supply of the stronger plant. They will then grow
on or next to their new best friend and can
survive for as long as their host does.

TIME TO GROW YOUR OWN

You don't need a garden or even any outdoor space to try growing your own plants – you can see nature in action with just a few simple household items. You will need an adult to help you with this activity.

Gather the following items:

- an egg
- a kitchen knife
- a piece of kitchen roll
- some cotton wool
- some cress seeds
- an eggcup

1) Ask an adult to cut the top off the egg and empty the contents – the shell will be your plant pot.

_____

2) Place a small piece of wet kitchen roll inside the shell, and then put wet cotton wool on top.

_____

3) Place your cress seeds on top of the damp cotton wool. Put your egg shell in the eggcup and leave it in a sunny place, watering the seeds again in a day or two.

_____

4) The cress should start to sprout in about two days and around a week later it should be tall enough to cut and use in salads and sandwiches!

FUN PLANT FACTS

The tallest living tree in the world is a coastal redwood called Hyperion. It is currently 115m (379ft) tall but it hasn't stopped growing yet...

Bamboo releases 30% more oxygen into the atmosphere than any other plant, making it one of the best natural air purifiers in the world!

The Rafflesia Arnoldii has the largest known flower in the world, but victory isn't sweet as this flower stinks of rotting flesh and is known as a corpse flower!

THE ANIMAL KINGDOM

Animals belong to the largest and most diverse category of living things – the animal kingdom. They can be found in almost every environment on the planet, from land to ocean and from ice to desert.

Unlike plants, most animals do not spend their lives in a state of continuous growth – a baby will grow into an adult and will then grow older rather than upwards. The oldest living land animal is believed to be Jonathan, a giant tortoise from St Helena, who is thought to have been born in 1832.

MARVELLOUS MAMMALS

Mammals are warm-blooded animals that have a backbone and are typically covered in hair or fur. They usually give birth to live young rather than lay eggs and they will produce and feed milk to their babies.

Humans, lions, bats and whales are all examples of mammals, though each is very different.

A female mammal can be pregnant for any period of time, ranging from 12 days for opossums to up to 22 months for elephants – that's nearly two years to wait before an elephant calf is born!

EXTRAORDINARY EGGS

Most reptiles and amphibians and all birds give birth by laying eggs.
Their babies develop inside fragile egg cases and remain there until
they are strong enough to break free, or hatch, on their own.

chicken egg

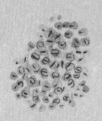

fish eggs

emu egg

Eggs come in all shapes, sizes, colours and patterns. We're probably most familiar with chicken eggs but did you know that fish can lay thousands of tiny eggs at a time or that emus lay gigantic dark green eggs?

———————

Female horn sharks lay spiral-shaped egg cases and a type of wading bird called a jacana lays speckled eggs, which are camouflaged amongst water weeds.

horn shark egg case

jacana egg

FROM THE TINIEST OF PACKAGES...

Although many animals start their lives within the shell of an egg, it is surprising just how big these hatchlings can grow! The largest living bird is the ostrich, a flightless giant that starts life in an egg that's just 15cm (5.9in) in diameter but can grow up to 2.8m (9.2ft) tall once hatched!

But if you want to see the biggest hatchlings ever, you'll have to go back to the age of the dinosaurs. The Apatosaurus egg is believed to have been 30cm (1ft) tall but, once hatched, this plant-eater could grow up to 26m (85ft) in length. That's one fast-growing dinosaur!

An adult Apatosaurus grew to be 5,000 times as heavy as its egg. If a chicken had the same growth pattern, an adult hen could weigh up to a quarter of a tonne (550lbs)!

EXCEPTIONS TO THE RULE

Now that we've learned how different kinds of animals reproduce, let's meet the rule-breakers!

Mammals that lay eggs instead of giving birth to live young are called monotremes. There are only a few monotremes left in the animal kingdom, including the platypus and some species of echidna (the spiny anteater).

There are some fish and reptiles that technically give birth to live young, as the eggs hatch inside the mother before they are born. These animals are called ovoviviparous and include some sharks, such as the basking shark, and some snakes, including the garter snake and pit viper.

Incredibly, the yellow-bellied three-toed skink of New South Wales, Australia, switches its birthing method depending on where it lives. If it is by the warm coast, it will lay eggs. If it is up in the mountains, it will incubate the eggs internally and then give birth to live young.

CH—CH—CHANGES

frogspawn

tadpole

tadpole with hind legs

Most baby animals look like miniature versions of their parents but there are some that make a more dramatic change as they enter into adulthood.

Tadpoles usually hatch from frogspawn and begin life looking like small black dots with tails. About four months later, after growing, changing colour and shedding their tails, the tadpoles transform into adult frogs!

young froglet   froglet   frog

The South American paradoxical frog breaks the usual rules of growth, by shrinking. Amazingly, it changes from a large tadpole to a much smaller frog!

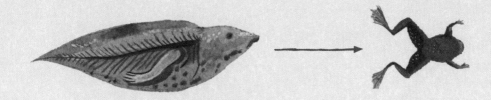

MUMMY MARSUPIALS

Marsupials, such as kangaroos, koalas and wombats, are a special type of mammal because the females have a built-in pouch to carry their young around. Baby marsupials, known as joeys, are born at a much earlier stage of development, which means they are more vulnerable and need a greater level of care than other animal new-borns.

Joeys live inside their mother's pouch for about six months until they are big enough to leave. However, kangaroo and wallaby joeys tend to stay in their pouches for a bit longer, despite being able to survive on their own. This means that their mother sometimes has to look after two joeys at once – one tiny baby and one fully developed!

cub

WHAT'S IN A NAME?

Most animals change their name as well as their appearance as they age. Common baby names include cub, calf, chick, kitten and puppy.

But have you heard of owlets, spiderlings and porcupettes? What about leverets (hares), cygnets (swans) and squabs (pigeons)? Baby names can be just as fascinating in the animal world as they are in the human one!

calf

chick

kitten (or kit)

puppy

baby and adult harp seal

baby and adult
langur monkey

baby and adult tapir

THE BEAUTY OF YOUTH

Some baby animals are born with special features to help them blend into their surroundings. For example, the harp seal uses its fluffy white fur to hide in the snow and the baby tapir's stripes help to conceal it in forests and long grasses.

Baby langur monkeys, however, are often a bright apricot colour for the first few weeks of life. Some biologists believe that this is so their parents can spot them if they go wandering off!

These distinctive markings disappear as the babies grow up and they can look after themselves without the need for childhood disguises.

BONUS FEATURES

Some baby animals develop new features as they grow older.

The echidna baby, or puggle, is completely hairless when it hatches and it lives in its mother's pouch for the first couple of months. Once it develops spines, the mother will gradually leave the puggle for longer periods of time until it can survive on its own, a process that will take about seven months.

echidna puggle

adult echidna

camel calf   adult camel

Surprisingly, the camel only develops its famous humps once it has
started on solid food, which can be any time after four months old.
Contrary to the popular myth, camel humps are not full of water!
Instead, they are made of fatty tissue that is used as an emergency
energy store for all those long desert walks.

BUT I DON'T WANT TO GROW UP!

The axolotl, also known as the Mexican walking fish, is a rare aquatic salamander with a youthful secret...

Nicknamed the Peter Pan of the animal kingdom, the axolotl is a neotenic species, which means that it usually does not age. Ordinarily amphibians develop from egg to larva to adult but not the axolotl.

These salamanders naturally lack the hormone that triggers adult development so, despite growing larger, they don't get any older biologically. For the axolotl, neoteny is genetic and so the whole species is kept in this child-like state but they are able to reproduce when ready.

THE EVOLUTION OF MAN

In 1859, naturalist Charles Darwin put forward a theory to explain the development of man. He argued that all life on Earth came from simpler, smaller life forms. These organisms then evolved to fit their environment, developing into the larger and more complex beings that we recognise today.

The similarity between man and chimpanzee is the perfect demonstration of evolution in action. Humans share 95-99% of their DNA with chimpanzees, who are our closest living relatives in the animal kingdom.

It took millions of years for humans to develop into what they are today. But as the world is in constant change, the next stage of man's evolution is yet to be decided...

THE UNIVERSE

There was a time when the heat of the Sun, the twinkle
of the stars and the earth beneath our feet did not exist.
The universe itself had an exciting and explosive beginning!

From the first rumblings of the Big Bang, our universe has been
expanding outwards, and over millions and even billions of years,
galaxies, stars, planets and moons have formed.

A VERY IMPORTANT EXPLOSION

Scientists believe that approximately 13.7 billion years ago, there was a very Big Bang! From this explosion, all the elements in the universe were created, but they were in one big messy mass.

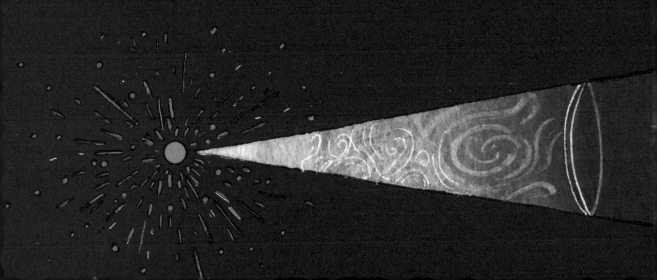

The outward force of the explosion and the dramatic cooling afterwards helped to form galaxies, and then gravity, stars, planets and comets followed.

OUR PLANET

The surface of the Earth has been through some huge changes since it was born. Perhaps the most noticeable of these changes is the movement of large bodies of land – the seven continents.

Around 200 million years ago, all the land on the planet was connected, much like a completed jigsaw. Then the heat from the Earth's core created currents underneath the surface and the large 'jigsaw pieces' (known as tectonic plates) began to disconnect and move apart, taking the land on the surface with them.

It took our planet millions of years to transform from one landmass called Pangea into the globe we now know, but it is not over yet...

———————

These tectonic plates are still in motion, moving two to ten centimetres (0.8–3.9in) every year. So there are more changes to come!

225 million
years ago

135 million
years ago

present day

MOVING MOUNTAINS

Mountains are formed by the movement of the top layer of the Earth, called the crust. This rocky layer is put under extreme pressure when tectonic plates move towards each other, and this pressure forces the plates upwards, creating a fold in the Earth's surface – and a mountain is born!

A chain of mountains is called a range.

The Himalayan mountain range of South Asia is an excellent example of fold-formed mountains. It is probably the most famous mountain range on Earth as it is home to nine of the ten highest peaks on the planet, including Mount Everest, the record-breaking 'roof of the world'!

In 1953, Edmund Hillary and Tenzing Norgay were the first people to scale Everest.

FLOW,
RIVER,
FLOW

The place where rivers begin is called the source, and they all travel downhill towards an ocean, sea, lake or larger river.

The point at which a river meets its final destination is called the mouth of the river.

Rivers typically get wider the further they travel as more water joins from streams and smaller rivers, known as tributaries.

ISOLATED ISLANDS

An island is a piece of land surrounded by water and can be found in rivers, oceans or lakes. They vary in shape, size and climate, from the tropical Galapagos to icy Greenland!

Most islands were created by the movement of tectonic plates causing a piece of the mainland to break away. Others rose up out of the sea as a result of erupting underwater volcanoes and some were carved out of land by erosion or as a result of rising sea levels covering the lower land.

Finally, some man-made islands have been created by depositing sand and earth into waterways or by draining waterlogged areas.

This island is the result
of an underwater
volcano erupting.